S0-BJM-687

362.29 H 1999
Herscovitch, Arthur G.
Everything you need to know
about drug abuse. $17.95

WHITE RIVER LIBRARY

Johnson County Public Library
401 South State Street
Franklin, IN 46131

WITHDRAWN

Everything You Need to Know About

DRUG ABUSE

Many teens consider drinking alcohol and smoking cigarettes a rite of passage.

• THE NEED TO KNOW LIBRARY •

Everything You Need to Know About

DRUG ABUSE

Dr. Arthur G. Herscovitch

THE ROSEN PUBLISHING GROUP, INC.
NEW YORK

White River Library
Johnson County Public Library
1664 Library Boulevard
Greenwood, IN 46142

Published in 1998, 1999 by The Rosen Publishing Group, Inc.
29 East 21st Street, New York, NY 10010

Copyright © 1998, 1999 by The Rosen Publishing Group, Inc.

Revised Edition 1999

All rights reserved. No part of this book may be reproduced in any form without permission in writing from the publisher, except by a reviewer.

Library of Congress Cataloging-in-Publication Data

Herscovitch, Arthur, 1947—
  Everything you need to know about drug abuse / Arthur G. Herscovitch—rev. ed.
  p.   cm.—(The need to know library)
  Includes bibliographical references and index.
  Summary: Provides information on drugs and their harmful effects, as well as how to avoid drugs and where to get help for drug abuse problems.
    ISBN 0-8239-3036-x
    1. Drug abuse—United States—Juvenile literature. 2. Drug abuse—United States—Prevention—Juvenile literature. 3. Teenagers—Drug abuse—United States—Juvenile literature. [1. Drug abuse.] I. Title. II. Series.
  HV5809.5.H49 1998
  362.29′0973—dc21
                                    97-49430
                                          CIP
                                          AC

Manufactured in the United States of America

Contents

Introduction

Lenny is more scared than he's ever been in his life. He has just been caught smoking marijuana with some friends behind the A&P. Lenny waits nervously as the manager calls his parents and the police. What is going to happen to him? How did he ever end up here?

Lenny has two siblings: his older sister, Donya, who is superpopular and totally brilliant, and his younger brother, Tomas, a star lacrosse player. Lenny has never stood out in any way at school—his grades have been mostly mediocre, he has always had trouble making friends, and he's never been much of an athlete.

Last summer Lenny met Adrian at Dino's Arcade. The two boys hit it off right away and started spending a lot of time together at the arcade and at the mall.

One day Adrian, along with several older guys, offered Lenny some pot. Lenny had never tried it, but he wanted to look cool, so he accepted. At first the drug just gave him a headache, but after a few more hits, Lenny began to feel high. Using pot seemed exciting to Lenny: No one in his family used drugs, and none of them knew about his secret. For a while Lenny felt special.

Since November Lenny has been smoking pot every day with his new "friends." Now, five months later, he is already suffering because of his choices: His grades are falling quickly, and some days he skips school altogether. Now Lenny may be in trouble with his parents—and the police. He has every reason to be scared.

Drug abuse among teenagers is a major problem in the United States. Surveys show that the number of teen drug users has risen steadily throughout the 1990s. Although this rate appears to be slowing down, the numbers are still high. Almost half of the high school seniors interviewed for a 1998 study said that they had tried marijuana.

Maybe you are curious about drugs. Perhaps, like Lenny, you feel that using drugs could be a way to make or keep new friends. Maybe you are using drugs now. Whatever the case, this book provides information about drugs and their harmful effects. It also discusses how to avoid using drugs, or if you are already using them, how to stop. Many teens either don't believe in or don't care about the dangers of smoking, drinking, and using drugs. This book can help you to see that drugs only get in the way of life. They keep you from experiencing all the truly good things that life has to offer.

All drugs can have negative effects on the body.

Chapter 1

Defining Drugs

A drug is any substance you take—whether it is man-made or from a natural source—that changes the way you think, feel, or act. Certain drugs are legal; within this category, some substances require a prescription, whereas others can be bought over-the-counter. A few drugs are legal but have certain limitations; in the United States, for example, there are minimum ages for the legal use of both alcohol and tobacco products.

Some common foods and drinks contain potentially dangerous drugs. For example, coffee, tea, soda, and chocolate contain caffeine. In addition, certain household products such as glue and cleaning supplies can be used improperly to produce druglike effects on the body.

All drugs can be harmful: legal drugs that are taken for too long or in too large a dosage, medicines used without a prescription, or illegal drugs used to get high. And legal or not, any drug can be abused, and most can lead to dependence. Drug abuse can cause many physical and psychological problems. This chapter discusses different types of drugs and the short- and long-term effects that they can have on your body and mind.

Alcohol

Since alcohol often causes a loss of inhibition—that is, it makes you act more spontaneous and less shy—many people think of it as a stimulant. But alcohol is actually a depressant. It slows down the heart rate as well as the central nervous system. Alcohol is absorbed into the bloodstream and is carried throughout the body. It can impair coordination and memory and dull the senses.

Millions of Americans, including teens, abuse alcohol. Even though purchasing alcohol is illegal for anybody under twenty-one, many teens have easy access to it. Alcohol is usually the first drug that teens try, and many are unaware of its harmful effects. Binge drinking (consuming large amounts of alcohol in a short period of time) is especially dangerous, as it can cause alcohol poisoning, coma, and death. It is a growing problem among teens and college students.

Caffeine

Caffeine is probably the most popular drug in the world. Between 82 and 92 percent of Americans drink coffee. Caffeine is a stimulant that affects the central nervous system and makes users feel more alert. It increases heart rate and blood pressure, and in large doses, caffeine can lead to anxiety and stomach problems. One dose of "stay awake" drugs like NoDoz and Vivarin contains about the same amount of caffeine as two cups of coffee.

Depressants

Depressants are among the most popular drugs in the United States. They are prescribed to treat people who suffer from anxiety, insomnia (sleeplessness), and excessive stress. When used correctly and under a doctor's care and supervision, depressants like Valium and Xanax can safely help many people.

But some people abuse these drugs. The effects of depressants are similar to those of alcohol. Users feel euphoric, or happy, at first but then become sleepy and begin to slur their speech. The eyes become lazy and have difficulty focusing. Depressants can pose great risks to both legal and illegal users. In addition, depressants often lead to dependence and addiction.

Hallucinogens

Hallucinogens, which are some of the illegal drugs most commonly abused by teens, include LSD (acid), PCP (angel dust), marijuana, mushrooms, and mescaline. When someone takes a hallucinogen, his or her sense of time and place becomes distorted. In other words, a user sees, hears, and feels things that aren't really there. Hallucinogens increase heart rate and blood pressure. They impair muscle

Depressants can be used safely to help treat anxiety and insomnia. Abusing them, however, can be life-threatening.

coordination and pain awareness and can cause insomnia. People high on hallucinogens often put themselves and others in danger by taking unreasonable risks or by acting violently or in unexpected ways. The effects of hallucinogens are very unpredictable and can last for up to twelve hours. In addition, some hallucinogens, including LSD and PCP, can lead to flashbacks.

Marijuana

Marijuana, commonly known as weed, pot, and grass, is the most popular hallucinogen among teens. According to a 1998 study, almost half of the high school seniors interviewed said that they had tried it. Like other hallucinogens, marijuana increases heart rate and distorts a person's sense of his or her surroundings. It also causes memory loss and can make a person feel paranoid, or irrationally suspicious of others.

Over time marijuana can damage the respiratory system, causing breathing problems and possibly lung or mouth cancer. It can also harm the immune system, which protects the body from disease and illness. In addition, for many people marijuana acts as a gateway drug, meaning that its use opens the door to the possibility of trying more dangerous substances like cocaine or heroin.

Ecstasy and Special K

Ecstasy (MDMA) and Special K (ketamine hydrochloride) are two hallucinogens that are becoming increasingly popular among teens. These drugs are often used at "raves," all-night underground parties, because they keep users awake and energized throughout the night.

Ketamine hydrochloride is an anesthetic (substance used to numb the body) used legally by veterinarians and doctors during surgery. But on the street, Special K is illegal to buy, use, or sell. Unfortunately most veterinarians don't usually lock up the drug, so it is easily accessible to burglars.

Special K and ecstasy users experience intense hallucinations and distorted senses. Both drugs also cause impaired judgment and coordination, which can lead to serious accidents. And since Special K and ecstasy prevent users from feeling pain, people high on these drugs can hurt themselves without even knowing it.

Inhalants

Inhalants are substances that are sniffed (inhaled through the nose). Most of these chemicals were never meant to be used to produce psychoactive (mind-altering) effects. Inhalants include model airplane glue, nail polish remover, gasoline, plastic cement, and lighter fluid. Inhalants are also found in many cleaning products.

These chemicals are easy to buy and use, but even a one-time use can be fatal. Inhalants increase heart rate, making the user feel dizzy and light-headed. They can also lead to asphyxia, which means that the flow of oxygen to the brain is stopped. This can cause a user to become unconscious.

Other consequences of inhalant use include nausea, lack of coordination, and decreased heart rate. Deep inhaling or heavy use can lead to violent behavior and breathing problems, and highly concentrated inhalants can cause heart attacks and suffocation. Over time a user's brain, lungs, liver, and kidneys can also suffer serious damage.

Narcotics

These drugs, which include heroin, opium, methadone, and morphine, are painkillers. Like depressants, narcotics slow down the central nervous system. Narcotics are among the most addictive drugs because they are very potent and have a heavy impact on the body and mind. At first, users feel euphoric and drowsy. But dangerous effects follow, such as breathing problems, convulsions, coma, and possible death. The withdrawal symptoms are severe and include tremors, cramps, chills, and sweating.

Heroin users face additional risks because they usually take the drug by injection. An infected user can pass deadly diseases like HIV to another user if the needle is not disinfected between uses. There are two main methods of injection: "skin-popping," or injecting the drug under the skin, and "mainlining," or injecting the substance directly into a vein.

Nicotine

Nicotine is found in cigarettes, cigars, and chewing tobacco. Since 1998 it has been illegal for anyone under the age of eighteen to buy or use these and other tobacco products. Some people smoke cigarettes to reduce tension, but nicotine actually increases heart rate and blood pressure. Like marijuana, the nicotine in tobacco products is considered a gateway drug. Studies show that teens are starting to smoke at a younger age than ever before.

Smoking increases the risks of heart disease; emphysema; stroke; and cancer of the mouth, throat, lungs, uterus, and bladder. Cigarettes are extremely addictive and contain many harmful chemicals, including gases that stick to the insides of the lungs.

Steroids

Some diseases, such as anemia, are treated safely and successfully by steroids. But these drugs are often used illegally. Athletes in particular use them unlawfully to heighten performance, since steroids make their bodies bigger, stronger, and faster.

But steroids can cause many health problems, including liver tumors, high blood pressure, and severe acne. Steroid users also experience periods of extreme paranoia, anger, and hallucinations. Long-term use can cause liver disease, cancer, and heart attacks.

Stimulants

Stimulants include street drugs like cocaine, crack, and amphetamines as well as prescription drugs such as Benzedrine and Dexedrine. Stimulants increase blood pressure and heart rate, making users feel euphoric and alert at first. This explains why amphetamines are often called pep pills. Later, however, users can suffer from hallucinations, convulsions, and even death. Many abusers become violent, anxious, and depressed, often losing interest in food and sex. Other dangerous effects include heart attacks, strokes, and respiratory failure.

This is a brief look at some of the most commonly abused drugs. Teens start using drugs for many different reasons—to fit in with friends, to experiment, or to rebel. Some just like the high. But no matter what your friends tell you, drugs can get you in trouble. Using them can ruin all aspects of your life.

Chapter 2

How Does It Begin?

Karla and Rena have been friends since second grade. They enjoy many of the same things, like writing poetry and painting, and they work together on the school paper and the yearbook.

One night when the two girls were over at Rena's house, Rena brought out some mushrooms that she had found in her older sister, Natalie's, room. Natalie had come home for Thanksgiving several weeks earlier and had confided to Rena that she and her new college friends had tried drugs. Natalie had said that magic mushrooms were her favorite because they made her feel really creative.

Now Rena dared Karla to try a mushroom with her, claiming that they could write some amazing poetry while they tripped. Karla and Rena shared a mushroom and sat up to write.

After a few minutes Karla found that she couldn't focus

Many teens use a drug because they think it will make them more creative.

long enough to write anything. All she could think about was how fast her heart seemed to be beating and how queasy she felt. Rena was writing a lot, but all Karla could do was try to keep from vomiting.

The next morning Karla still felt confused. She picked up Rena's notebook, but all she saw were pages and pages of meaningless scribbles. So much for creativity, thought Karla.

There are many reasons why teens might use drugs. This chapter looks at some of the most common ones.

Experimentation

When something is forbidden, many teens want to try it even more, especially if their parents are the ones saying, "Don't do that." Everyone rebels against an authority figure at some point in life. It's one way to find out who you are and to create your own identity. In addition, using drugs can be an especially tempting way to rebel because they promise to make you feel good.

Many teens believe that they are expanding their horizons or increasing their creativity by experimenting with drugs. But most teens don't think about the harmful effects drug use can have on all areas of the body. Trying drugs just to see what they feel like can be very dangerous and can lead to serious long-term problems in your life.

Pop Culture Influences

Most likely you've heard about drugs. Television, radio,

and newspapers are filled with stories of movie stars, musicians, and athletes who use drugs. Popular movies such as *Trainspotting* and *Pulp Fiction* feature characters that use drugs. Movies often glamorize drug use and they have a strong influence on teens' view of drugs. Teens may underestimate the danger of drugs and mimic the actions that they see and hear. This is how some teens start taking drugs.

The most common drugs that teens first try are nicotine (cigarettes) and alcohol. Because these drugs are legal, many teens may not understand their harmful effects. Worse, some studies show that once a person tries one drug, he or she is usually willing to try other, more harmful drugs.

Dealing with Problems

If a person tries a drug and likes how it makes him or her feel, there's a good chance that the person will continue to use the drug. Being a teen isn't always easy. You may feel that your parents don't understand you, or that school is boring and a waste of time. You may be feeling depressed about your life or upset about a family problem. If you try a drug and it eases your pain or relieves your unhappiness, you may start using drugs regularly in an effort to cope with your situation. But in the end, the drug use will only make those problems worse.

Parents Who Drink or Use Drugs

Some teens grow up in homes where they often see their

Teens are surrounded by images that glamorize drug use.

It can be hard to resist the temptation to try drugs, especially when your peers are using them.

parents drink alcohol or use other drugs. Some parents may use alcohol responsibly, as many people do. But many others have problems with alcohol or drugs. Teens with substance-abusing parents may believe that drugs and alcohol are acceptable ways to cope with problems. They have learned this behavior from their parents.

Another risk factor is the fact that studies show that children of substance abusers are at higher risk than children whose parents don't have problems with drugs or alcohol. But, while these children are at higher risk for alcohol or drug-abuse problems, according to most studies today, genetic factors alone do not cause severe problems. Although scientists continue to conduct studies looking for specific genes that cause certain behaviors, they believe that abuse and addiction involve a combination of several factors. Still, children of substance abusers are not out of danger. Those who develop substance abuse problems of their own do so at an earlier age. Their problems tend to be more severe, as well.

Peer Pressure

The most common reason that people start using and continue to use drugs is influence from friends. You may find that a lot of what your friends do has an effect on you. If a teen is part of a group which values drug use, it can be pretty hard not to use drugs, and still feel accepted by people in that group.

Other teens may feel alone and left out of a group. Wanting to fit in or look cool to others, they start using drugs. It's hard to deal with peer pressure because it can be very subtle. In other words, many teens may not realize or recognize when they're succumbing to peer pressure. It can feel very natural to take a hit off a joint or have a beer when hanging out with friends. But soon these activities become a regular occurrence, and then you don't feel comfortable not using when you're with your friends. Your friends may make you feel unwelcome if you don't participate in their drug use.

Dealer Pressure

Many teens know of dealers in their school or on their street. Sometimes a dealer targets certain people and offers them drugs free or for very little money. The dealer wants a person to become hooked, and then buy drugs at a much higher cost. In this way, the dealer can make a lot of money. Some dealers can be very convincing, and teens find it difficult to resist the pressure.

The important thing to remember throughout this book is that all the drugs described here are addictive. You can easily become "hooked" on them, and once you're hooked, it's hard to stop.

Chapter 3

Problems Caused by Drug Abuse

From what you've read so far, you know that any drug that changes how a person thinks and feels can be harmful. Drugs may cause physical, psychological, and legal problems. This chapter will look closely at those specific problems.

Physical Problems

The physical problems that drugs cause may be divided into three groups. These are loss of physical coordination, violence, and illness.

Loss of Physical Coordination

Physical coordination means your ability to control your movements. Some drugs have a harmful effect on this ability. For example, alcohol, marijuana, depressants, narcotics, and inhalants can slow your reaction time. These drugs also weaken your control over your muscles. Being high on any of these drugs can be very dangerous. It is not safe for you to drive a car, operate machinery, or be involved in any other activity that requires good coordination. Anyone high on these drugs increases the chances of having accidents or hurting him- or herself and others.

Violence

Certain drugs cause users to become violent toward others. For example, cocaine, crack, and amphetamines can make people become very angry easily. This anger often leads to violence. Steroids frequently cause people to become aggressive, so someone using these drugs may often get into arguments and fights. This state, called "roid rage," is very scary because the user loses control over his or her emotions. Sometimes drugs even cause people to become violent toward themselves. When people come down after being high on cocaine or amphetamines, they often enter a deep depression. They may even attempt suicide.

Illness

Drugs damage your body and can cause many types of illness:

- Alcohol can cause cirrhosis and cancer of the liver.
- Cigarettes can cause ulcers, bronchitis, emphysema, heart disease, and many forms of cancer.

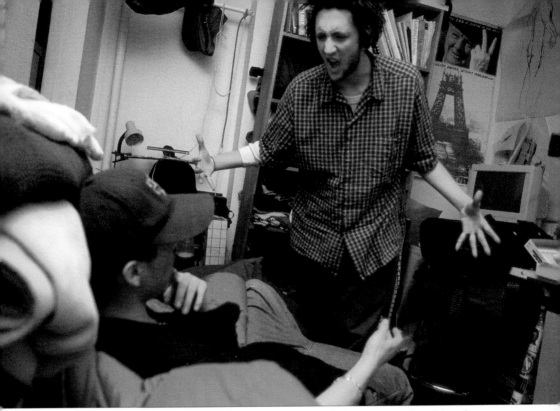

Some drugs will cause a user to become violent toward a friend or family member.

- Hallucinogens can cause heart and lung failure and convulsions.
- Inhalants can cause abdominal pain, brain damage, and hepatitis.
- Stimulants can cause heart attack, stroke, brain seizure, and respiratory failure.

Drugs also lower your immune system, which helps fight illness and disease. In addition, many drug abusers don't take care of themselves. To them, drugs are more important than food or sleep.

Inhibitions

Many drugs lower your inhibitions. Inhibitions are

Some teens may do things they wouldn't normally do while on drugs.

internal warning signals that help you decide what you feel comfortable doing. If those inhibitions are taken away, a person may be more likely to try other drugs, engage in criminal behavior, or have unprotected sex. Drugs affect your ability to weigh the consequences of your actions. You may find yourself dealing with a jail sentence, an unwanted pregnancy, or a sexually transmitted disease.

AIDS (Acquired Immunodeficiency Syndrome)
In this age of HIV and AIDS, people who use injected drugs such as heroin are at a very high risk of contracting the HIV virus. This is because needles are often shared among users and are not properly cleaned between uses. The virus is easily transmitted from one person to another through small amounts of blood left on the needle.

If you use injected drugs or have unprotected sex, you will have a high risk of becoming infected. HIV and AIDS have spread at incredible rates. In 1998, 15 percent of all new infections occurred in young people between the ages of thirteen and twenty-four. There is no cure for AIDS yet, even though millions of dollars are spent every year to find drugs that slow down the harmful effects of the virus.

Psychological Problems
Drugs affect how you think and feel. Drug abuse causes several types of mental and emotional problems, including loss of interest in things, memory problems, guilt and depression, anxiety, and denial.

Drug abuse can cause many psychological problems, such as depression.

For example, drug abuse causes a loss of interest in school, sports, and other social activities. Drug abusers often show apathy. This means a loss of interest in everything—except drugs. Many abusers drop out of school or lose their jobs. You may know someone who went to school with you, got into drugs, and then dropped out.

Denial

Most drug abusers don't think they have a problem. They may feel bad, or guilty about their behavior, but they have no idea how to stop it. To cover up feelings of isolation and guilt, many abusers deny their problems.

Denial is a defense mechanism that many abusers use to continue their drug abuse. To admit their problems means that they have to do something about the problems. This is a very difficult realization for drug abusers to make. Instead of admitting their problems, they make up excuses and blame others for them.

Do I Have a Problem?

Here are some questions to ask yourself if you think you might have a problem with drugs and alcohol:

1. Do you use drugs on a regular basis?
2. Are drugs important to you?
3. Do you use drugs when you are alone?
4. Do you use drugs to help you relax or escape your problems?

5. Do you worry if you can't get drugs?

6. Do you mix drugs to get a stronger, more intense high?

7. Do you seek out parties and places where people are using drugs?

8. Have you lied to your family or friends to cover up your drug use?

9. Do you arrange your life around getting high?

10. Do you believe you can control your drug use?

11. Do you get high even when you promise yourself you won't?

12. Do you get angry when people say you have a drug problem?

If you've answered yes to more than three of these questions, there could be a serious problem. You should consider seeking help for drug abuse.

Legal Problems

Teens abusing drugs often don't care about anything else. Drugs cause them to become indifferent to their lives. Stealing and abusing drugs is against the law. If you are caught taking drugs or stealing money to buy them, you are risking your future.

Because of the rise in crime by young people, many courts are giving harsher punishments to juveniles. Even if you are under eighteen, you may face jail time for drug abuse. Having a criminal record can hurt your chances of being admitted to college or getting a job.

Here are a couple of questions to ask yourself: If you are a person who doesn't use drugs, are you thinking about using them? If you are thinking about using them, what are your reasons? What do you know about drugs? If you are already using drugs, are they causing problems in your life? What were the reasons you started using them in the first place?

If teens use drugs when they are alone, it is usually a warning sign for drug abuse.

Chapter 4

From Abuse to Addiction

Many drug counselors and former drug addicts say that nobody makes a decision to become addicted to drugs or alcohol. It isn't a conscious decision. In other words, nobody plans to become addicted to drugs and alcohol. If you're abusing drugs, it can happen without your realizing it. The longer you use drugs, the more you need them. Soon drugs take control over your life, and you find you can't stop using.

Tolerance

If you continue taking drugs, your body soon develops a tolerance to them. Tolerance means that you need to use more and more of the drug to get the original effect. For example, at first, a couple of drinks may be all you need to feel good. But soon you find that you need much more than that to get the same feeling. Maybe you need to mix drugs to feel high. This is even more dangerous, because many abusers are unaware of the reactions their bodies may have to taking combinations of certain drugs. In this case, there is a higher risk of overdose.

Some abusers take other drugs to relieve withdrawal symptoms. For example, people addicted to heroin may take depressants to ease their discomfort when they come off heroin. A person's tolerance becomes higher and higher the longer he or she abuses drugs, which increases the threat of addiction.

What is Drug Addiction?

Drug addiction has two parts. One is psychological addiction, and the other is physical addiction. Both aspects make it very difficult to stop using drugs.

Psychological Addiction

Psychological addiction is needing to use a drug in order to feel normal. You need a drug to function and feel good. For example, you may feel that you cannot have fun at a party unless you're drunk or high. Or you may believe that the only way for you to mellow out is to smoke a joint.

If you cannot wait to use drugs, or if you think a lot about using, you are psychologically addicted. You want to be high or drunk as often as you can. You may show up at work or school under the influence of drugs. You may use drugs while you're at school or work. Drugs are always in the back of your mind. Much of your lifestyle revolves around using drugs or alcohol.

Physical Addiction

Physical addiction is when your body needs a drug in order to function. If you stop using the drug, your body goes into withdrawal. The body becomes accustomed to the drug, and the addict, without the drug, feels sick and experiences one or more of the following symptoms: nausea, sweating, confusion, depression, insomnia, chills, cramps, and disorientation. Withdrawal from depressants is especially dangerous. If abusers try to quit without the proper medical treatment, they risk death.

The Stages of Addiction

As a person becomes addicted to a drug, he or she goes through four stages. For some people, it takes several years to go through these stages. Others go through them in a few months. This is because it is easier to become addicted to some drugs than others. Crack and heroin are drugs that a person can become addicted to very easily, even after using them only one or two times.

Stage I

At first, you begin using a drug here and there, and mainly for fun. You basically do it because your friends do. You don't have any major problems because of your drug use. There are other things in your life like hobbies, sports, or school. Your drug use doesn't yet interfere with these activities. Some people always stay at this stage. Many teens go through a stage of experimenting with

Withdrawal symptoms are the major factor behind physical addiction.

drugs, and then they stop. Others, however, really like what drugs do for them. They end up using more and more. When this happens, they move into the second stage, which brings them closer to addiction.

Stage II

Now you find yourself needing more of the drug because your tolerance has increased. Small amounts are not good enough. It takes more to make you high or drunk. In order to increase the high, you begin using other drugs. For example, most drug users start with alcohol. Some use marijuana. In this second stage, it's not uncommon to try drugs like LSD, cocaine, or ecstasy. You find yourself thinking about drugs, even when you are not using.

Drugs start to interfere with school or work. You lose interest in school and you cut class. If you're working, you may be late, miss work, and eventually get fired from your job. You no longer hang out with friends who don't use or drink. You mainly want to be with using or drinking friends. A lot of your money goes toward buying drugs. Things that used to interest you no longer do. You also find yourself feeling more uptight and suspicious. You argue more with people, especially your family. Addiction is starting to set in.

Stage III

By now, drugs are more important than just about anything else. It takes large amounts to get high or drunk.

This costs money. You may start selling drugs as a way of getting money. You may do other illegal things to get money. Some drug abusers turn to prostitution to get drugs.

During this stage, most drug abusers have dropped out of school or lost their jobs. Many leave home or get kicked out. If you're still living at home, there is a lot of arguing. Drug withdrawal occurs. You feel a lot of depression and anger, and you're always uptight. The only way to make these feelings go away is to use more drugs. But the depression and anger always return.

Stage IV

Your drug use is completely out of control. Nothing else is important to you. Your body is so used to drugs that it is hard to get a high. Anger, suspicion, and depression are with you every day. Whenever you come down from drugs, the feelings are there.

Physically and mentally, you feel very run down. Thoughts of suicide come and go. You've had trouble with the law. Maybe you've even been arrested. It's hard to get money for drugs. You will do anything you have to to get drugs. When you run out of them, withdrawal is terrible. Some people make suicide attempts and end up in the hospital. Some people end up in jail. At this point, addiction must be treated with medical and psychological help. If it is not treated properly, addiction can result in death.

Can't I Just Stop Using?

It is easier to stop using drugs in the first stage, and harder in the second. Once you are in the third or fourth stage of addiction, it is very hard to stop.

When you are addicted to drugs, you are trapped in the drug cycle. You use a drug to get a high (to feel good). But problems often occur; arguments, fights, no money, quitting school, losing a job, depression, anger, guilt, etc. You use more drugs to get rid of these feelings. More problems occur, and so on. Some people feel trapped in their drug use. They feel hopeless. They believe there is no escape. If you are feeling trapped in your drug use, you may believe that no one can help you. But there is help. Many people find the help they need and recover. The next chapter will tell you what happens in recovery and how to stay away from drugs altogether.

Chapter 5

Quitting Drugs

Both drug abuse and drug addiction cause serious problems for people. But even though they have problems from their drug abuse, many people don't want to quit. For them, the good feelings caused by drugs are more important. They are willing to experience problems from drugs, because nothing outweighs the high. The drug is the most important thing in their lives. They continue to use and use, and get into more and more trouble. Many die from their drug abuse. They may overdose, commit suicide, or die from an illness or violence caused by drugs.

Other individuals enjoy the high feelings from drugs, but they don't want the problems. They try to cut back on their drug use. These people hope to avoid problems by using less. They try to use small amounts of a drug. They try to use drugs only when they think it is safe to do so. They say to themselves that they won't use drugs before or during school. They say that they will control how much they take. But it can be very difficult to control drug use. In the worst case, drugs take away any control you have over your life.

Some people are in Stage II of drug use. They abuse drugs, but they are not yet addicted. They may be successful in cutting back. You may promise yourself that you'll only use small amounts of a drug. You may say to yourself that you'll only use drugs at certain times. Or maybe you try a different drug and think you won't have a problem with it. This might work for a time. But soon, your drug use will sneak up on you. Gradually, you'll use more and more. Soon, you'll be using the same amount that you promised yourself you wouldn't use. Maybe you'll use more than ever before.

Why Do People Stop Using Drugs?

Many people stop using drugs. They come to realize that the high is not worth the problems caused by their drug abuse. They finally see that drugs cause more harm than they are worth. Some people have to hit rock bottom before they realize they have a problem. Maybe they are arrested. Or maybe they lose a job, or get kicked out of school. Maybe they end up at a hospital. Sometimes they lose a boyfriend or girlfriend because of their drug abuse.

If you abuse drugs, and there are people who care about you, they may hold an intervention. They and a counselor meet with you and force you into treatment. It is not because they are mean. It is not because they are trying to control you. It is because they care. Sometimes an intervention is done by a parent. Sometimes it is done by a teacher or a school principal. Sometimes the courts intervene and sentence you to drug treatment.

You may voluntarily try to quit using drugs, or you may be forced into quitting. Either way, it takes hard work and dedication to stay straight. Some people are able to stop using drugs on their own. They decide to quit, and they stick with it. Others need help. For these people, treatment programs are available. Some treatment programs are outpatient. This means that you visit the treatment program a few times a week for a few months. Other programs are inpatient. This means that you live in the treatment building while you receive treatment.

Treatment for Drug and Alcohol Abuse

People in treatment go through four stages. The first stage is coming off of drugs. Some people come off of drugs without too much trouble. However, others go into drug withdrawal. This often happens with people who have been using drugs for a long time. Drug withdrawal makes them feel sick. Different drugs produce different types of withdrawal symptoms.

For example, withdrawal from cocaine usually causes a person to feel depressed, nervous, and very uptight.

Friends can help a drug abuser realize there is a problem and urge him or her to get help.

Sometimes the person becomes suicidal. Withdrawal from narcotics causes people to sweat, feel sick to the stomach, and shake. Other drugs have other uncomfortable effects. Some drugs are easier to quit. Other drugs have withdrawal that can be severe enough to cause death. That is why treatment programs have doctors to help people come off of drugs safely.

Once drug withdrawal is over, the individual enters the second stage of treatment. It is here that the person is helped to really accept that he or she has a problem with drugs. Remember that most drug users are in denial. They like the high so much that they refuse to believe that drugs cause problems. Treatment helps people look at drugs for what they really are.

There are many groups that allow members to share their experiences and support each other as they quit drugs.

People use drugs because they like how drugs make them feel. They don't use drugs to have problems. But trouble does occur. This usually causes the drug abuser to feel guilty and depressed. To get rid of these feelings, the person uses even more. When people stop using drugs, they have to face and solve their problems. They also have to deal with all sorts of uncomfortable feelings caused by these problems.

The third stage of treatment helps people deal with these feelings. It also helps them sort out their problems and to find solutions. By now, the person in treatment is starting to feel a little better. But there is more to do. People who give up drugs, but don't make changes in how they live, usually start to use again. This is called a relapse.

During the last (fourth) stage of treatment, the person learns to make friends with people who don't use. He or she learns how to have a life without drugs.

Self-Help Groups

If you are committed to quitting and have taken the first steps to recovery, you can stay off drugs. It's important to remember, however, that an abuser also needs to enter a recovery program. Groups such as Alcoholics Anonymous and Narcotics Anonymous offer help. Their programs give patients tools to deal with recovery. Patients learn new types of behavior and receive support from others who have had similar experiences.

These twelve-step programs teach their members that drug and alcohol addiction are ongoing problems.

One of the best ways to stay away from drugs is to have drug-
free friends.

There is no cure. Recovery is a continuing process that takes much work. These programs give members the support they need to stay drug-free. But the members must also come to terms with many things.

The Twelve-Step Philosophy

In a twelve-step program, members:

- admit that their lives have got out of control
- believe that they can change and get better
- agree to work with others to change their behavior
- make a list of destructive behaviors as well as positive qualities
- share the list with a trusted person
- decide to leave old behaviors and attitudes in the past
- work at changing old behaviors and attitudes
- recognize those who have been hurt by their behavior and apologize to them
- take responsibility for their problems and forgive themselves
- admit when they are wrong
- work on being a better person without drugs
- help others

Studies show that those who participate in self-help groups have a higher success rate at staying drug-free. Overall, the programs help people take control of their lives and give them the power to make positive changes.

Chapter 6

Staying Straight

It's not always easy to stay away from drugs. Sometimes the pressure to use can be pretty heavy. You have to make some tough choices in your life. In the process, though, you may learn how much you care about yourself and your future. You may find that respecting yourself means staying drug-free.

Why Is It So Hard?

If you use drugs, there's a pretty good chance that your friends also use drugs. Most of what you do with your friends probably involves drugs. When you stop using drugs, your friends may put pressure upon you to change your mind. They may not like your wanting to stay straight. They may not want to spend time with you unless you use with them. In other words, these so-called friends may not respect your desire to quit drugs.

If you don't have any nonusing friends, you may feel very much alone.

Most major cities have support groups for teens who want to quit. These teens can meet others who are going through similar experiences and who can offer both friendship and support in staying straight.

To find a support group near you, talk to a school counselor or teacher. In addition, there are several organizations listed in the back of this book that can refer you to support groups in your area.

Stress

Most regular users come to rely upon drugs to help them handle stress. If they are feeling uptight, angry, or depressed, they use drugs to make these feelings go away. The unpleasant feelings usually return, but there are always more drugs to take.

If you use drugs regularly and decide to quit, you will have to learn alternative methods of dealing with stress. Most people do not stop using drugs until they run into serious problems. Of course, these problems cause stress. You will have to face and solve your problems without drugs, and that can be very difficult.

For example, let's say that while he was high, a person has hurt others who trusted and loved him by robbing or lying to them. He then makes the decision to stop using drugs, but feels guilty about how he has acted in the past. He knows that he has to apologize to these people. That isn't easy to do. It forces a person to

Individual therapy is a very useful tool when a person is recovering from a drug addiction.

confront feelings that cause shame and embarrassment. But it's a necessary part of starting a new, drug-free life.

There are many people around who can help you. The Where to Go for Help section at the end of this book is a good place to start.

Overconfidence

Some people believe that quitting drugs is easy. They are confident that everything will be fine and don't seek out people to support them in staying straight. They may even continue to hang out with drug-abusing friends. Before they know it, they are back to using.

If you are using drugs, and you decide to quit, try not to be overconfident. Do not be afraid to ask others for support. A willingness to accept help often makes the difference between staying straight and relapsing.

Because drugs are everywhere, it may seem as though they are harmless. You may even know some regular drug users who seem to be doing okay. The truth is that most of them are just putting on a front of having it together. In reality they are dealing with a lot of problems.

Choosing Your Friends

If you spend time with people who drink and use drugs, they will likely pressure you to do the same. They will tell you that using drugs is fun and that it won't cause you any harm. And they'll probably be pretty convincing. However, if you hang out with people who do not use drugs, you can avoid being hassled. Sometimes it may seem as if almost all teens use drugs, but that is not true. If you look around, you will find that many of your peers do not use. Having drug-free friends is your best defense against drug abuse.

It's Your Decision

Choosing not to use drugs or drink alcohol means that you have decided to maintain control over your life. You don't have to defend the decision to stay in control. If someone tries to pressure you to use or drink, he or she may be jealous of your self-control and may want to take away some of your power. It should be easy to see the weaknesses in this kind of person. If people in your

There are many other satisfying ways to spend your time that will enhance your life.

life make you feel that you need to defend your choice to stay straight, you have two options. You can make sure that you keep these individuals out of your life, or you can try to help them face their own drug or alcohol problems.

Dealing Without Drugs

Your teen years can be difficult. Everything around you and within you is changing, and it is normal to feel confused, angry, restless, and scared. Sometimes all you want to do is escape, and drugs may seem like your only choice.

The truth is that life offers an enormous variety of paths to choose from. There are plenty of activities that don't involve drugs that can give your life meaning. The trick is to try out as many different things as you can until you find some that you enjoy and feel confident about. Playing sports, making music, writing, painting, dancing—these are just a few examples of the hundreds of drug-free activities that can lift your spirits and expand your mind. Once you find something that challenges and rewards you, it will be easy to see through the empty promises that drugs and alcohol offer.

Glossary

addiction Dependence on a habit-forming substance so strong that its use causes physical and psychological problems.

asphyxia Loss of consciousness from lack of oxygen and excess of carbon dioxide in the blood.

central nervous system The part of the nervous system consisting of the brain and the spinal cord.

coma Deep unconsciousness from which a person cannot be roused; caused by disease or injury.

coordination Normal interaction of body parts, such as eyes and hands, for effective operation.

defense mechanism Mental process of the unconscious that enables a person to cope with painful problems.

denial Unconscious defense mechanism by which one refuses to admit painful thoughts, emotions, or facts.

disorientation Loss of an accurate sense of time, place, or one's own identity.

gene The unit of inheritance from parents of physical and mental traits.

hallucination Experience of unreal sights and sounds; caused by drug use or illness.

high State of elation or sense of power caused by use of a drug.

immune system Bodily system that protects the body from foreign invaders such as bacteria and viruses.

paranoia Mental disorder in which a person irrationally suspects others of having hostile intentions.

stress Bodily or mental tension created by outside circumstances or events.

For Further Reading

Adint, Victor. *Drugs and Crime*. Rev. ed. New York: Rosen Publishing Group, 1997.

Berger, Gilda. *Patty's Story: Straight Talk About Drugs*. Brookfield, CT: Millbrook Press, 1991.

Cheney, Glenn A. *Drugs, Teens, and Recovery: Real-Life Stories of Trying to Stay Clean*. Springfield, NJ: Enslow, 1993.

Clayton, Lawrence. *Coping with a Drug-Abusing Parent*. Rev. ed. New York: Rosen Publishing Group, 1995.

Folkers, Gladys. *Taking Charge of My Mind and Body: A Girl's Guide to Outsmarting Alcohol, Drugs, Smoking, and Eating Problems*. Minneapolis, MN: Free Spirit Publishing, 1997.

Glass, George. *Drugs and Fitting In*. New York: Rosen Publishing Group, 1998.

Grabish, Beatrice. *Drugs and Your Brain*. New York: Rosen Publishing Group, 1998.

Grosshandler, Janet. *Drugs and Driving*. Rev. ed. New York: Rosen Publishing Group, 1997.

Harris, Jacqueline L. *Drugs and Disease*. Rev. ed. Brookfield, CT: Twenty-First Century Books, Millbrook Press, 1995.

Hodgkinson, Liz. *Drug Abuse: Your Questions Answered.* New York: Sterling Publishing, 1996.

Hyde, Margaret O. *Know About Drugs.* 4th ed. New York: Walker Publishing, 1996.

Long, Susan, and Beth Marks. *Teens and Tobacco: A Fatal Attraction.* Brookfield, CT: Twenty-First Century Books, Millbrook Press, 1996.

Packard, Gwen. *Coping with Stress.* New York: Rosen Publishing Group, 1997.

Ryan, Elizabeth A. *Straight Talk About Drugs and Alcohol.* New York: Facts on File, 1995.

Siegel, Mark, ed. *Illegal Drugs and Alcohol: Hurting American Society.* 3rd ed. Wylie, TX: Information Plus, 1997.

Trautman, Neal E., and Lon Wilder. *Fifty Things Teens Can Do to Fight Drugs.* Winter Springs, FL: Standards and Training, 1991.

Where to Go for Help

In the United States

Al-Anon/Alateen Family Group Headquarters
1600 Corporate Landing Parkway
Virginia Beach, VA 23454-5617
(888) 4AL-ANON (425-2666)
Web site: http://www.al-anon.alateen.org

Alcoholics Anonymous World Services
P.O. Box 459
New York, NY 10163
(212) 870-3400
Web site: http://www.aa.org

American Council for Drug Education
164 West 74th Street
New York, NY 10023
(800) 488-DRUG (488-3784)
Web site: http://www.acde.org

Cocaine Anonymous World Services
P.O. Box 2000
Los Angeles, CA 90049-8000
(310) 559-5833
Web site: http://www.ca.org

Narcotics Anonymous
World Service Office
19737 Nordhoff Place
Chatsworth, CA 91311
(818) 773-9999
Web site: http://www.na.org

**National Clearinghouse for Alcohol and Drug
Information**
P.O. Box 2345
Rockville, MD 20847-2345

(800) 729-6686
Web site: http://www.health.org

National Council on Alcoholism and Drug Dependence
12 West 21st Street, 7th Floor
New York, NY 10010
(800) NCA-CALL (622-2255)
Web site: http://www.ncadd.org

Self-Help Clearinghouse
c/o Saint Clare's Health Services
25 Pocono Road
Denville, NJ 07834
(973) 625-7101
Web site: http://www.cmhc.com/selfhelp

In Canada

Addiction Research Foundation
1615 Dundas Street East, 2nd Floor
Whitby, Ontario L1N 2L1
(905) 576-6277
Web site: http://www.arf.org

Addictions Foundation of Manitoba–Youth Unit
200 Osborne Street
Winnipeg, Manitoba R3C 1V4
(204) 944-6200
Web site: http://www.afm.mb.ca

Alliance for a Drug-Free Canada
P.O. Box 355, Station A
North York, Ontario M5W 1C5
(416) 730-4670

Cocaine Anonymous–Toronto
2 Bloor Street West, Suite 276A

Toronto, Ontario M4W 3E2
Web site: http://www.interlog.com/~recovery
(416) 927-7858

Narcotics Anonymous
P.O. Box 5700, Depot A
Toronto, Ontario M5W 1P9
(416) 691-9519
Web site: http://www.na.org

Hotline Numbers

American Council for Drug Education Hotline
(800) DRUGHELP (378-4435)

The Cocaine Hotline
(800) COCAINE (262-2463)

**The National Drug and Treatment Referral
   Routing Service**
(800) 662-HELP (662-4357)

Teen Help Hotline
(800) 637-0701

National Youth Crisis Hotline
(800) HIT-HOME (448-4663)

Web Sites

Partnership for a Drug-Free America
http://www.drugfreeamerica.org

Teen Advice Network
http://www.teenadvice.net

Index

About the Author

Dr. Herscovitch is a clinical psychologist who has been on staff at the Addictions Foundation of Manitoba in Winnipeg, Manitoba, Canada, for twenty-two years. He also has a private practice and is an assistant professor of psychology at the School of Medicine at the University of Manitoba. Dr. Herscovitch received his Ph.D. in clinical psychology from the University of Manitoba. He has lectured on the topics of alcoholism and chemical dependency in both Canada and the United States.

Photo Credits

Cover by Christine Innamorato; pp. 2, 28, 34, 52 by Ira Fox; pp. 8, 21, 30 by Seth Dinnerman; p. 12 by Kathleen McClancy; pp. 18, 54 by Ethan Zindler; p. 22 by John Novajosky; p. 27 by Sara Friedman; p. 38 by Megan Alderson; pp. 46, 48 by Lauren Piperno.